MINI PETS

Beetles

By Theresa Greenaway
Photography by Chris Fairclough

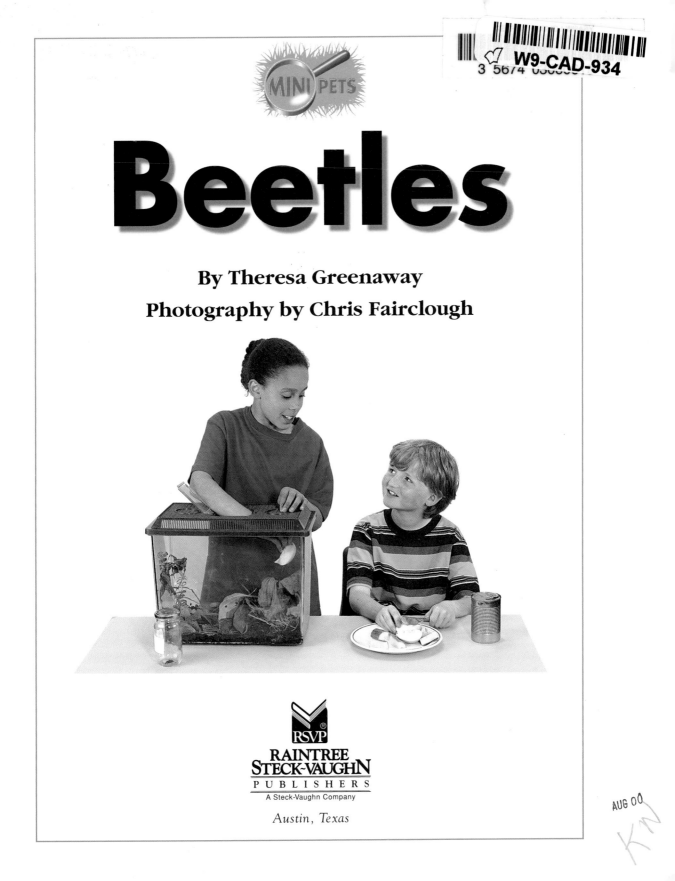

RSVP
RAINTREE
STECK·VAUGHN
PUBLISHERS
A Steck-Vaughn Company

Austin, Texas

Published by Raintree Steck-Vaughn Publishers, an imprint of Steck-Vaughn Company.

Acknowledgments
Project Editors: Gianna Williams, Kathy DeVico
Project Manager: Joyce Spicer
Illustrated by Jim Chanell and Stefan Chabluk
Designed by Ian Winton

Planned and produced by Discovery Books

Library of Congress Cataloging-in-Publication Data
Greenaway, Theresa, 1947–
Beetles/by Theresa Greenaway; photographs by Chris Fairclough.
p. cm. — (Minipets)
Includes bibliographical references (p. 30) and index.
Summary: Provides information on the identification, life cycle, and habitats of beetles, as well as on how to collect and care for them as pets.
ISBN 0-8172-5586-9 (hardcover)
ISBN 0-7398-1384-6 (softcover)
1. Beetles as pets — Juvenile literature. 2. Beetles — Juvenile literature.
[1. Beetles as pets. 2. Beetles. 3. Pets.] I. Fairclough, Chris, ill. II. Title.
III. Series: Greenaway, Theresa, 1947–   Minipets.
SF459.B43G074   1999
638' . 576 — dc21   98-34074
CIP   AC

1 2 3 4 5 6 7 8 9 0 LB 02 01 00 99
Printed and bound in the United States of America.
Words explained in the glossary appear in **bold** the first time they are used in the text.

WARNING

Some beetles bite. Other beetles have unpleasant, clinging smells.
A few types of beetles release chemicals that can blister human skin.

Contents

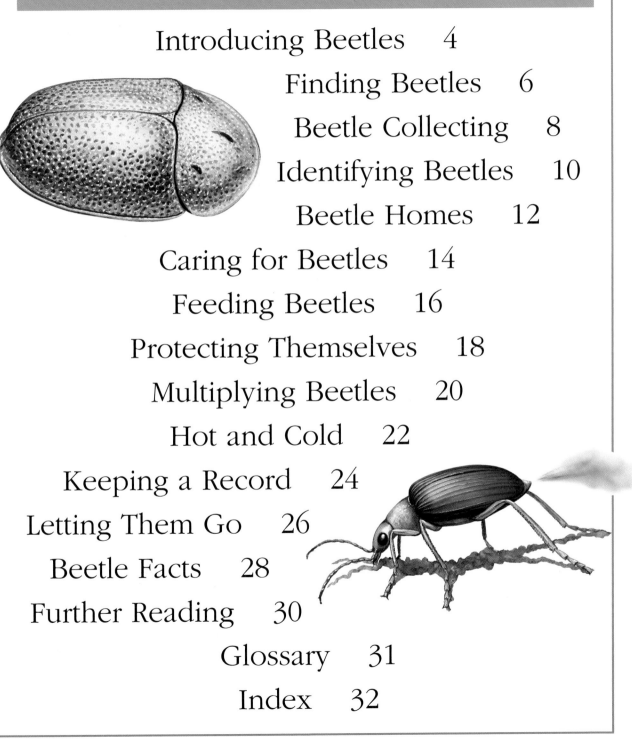

Introducing Beetles

There are millions and millions of beetles in the world. In fact, beetles represent one-fourth of the entire animal kingdom! Many kinds of beetles make great minipets, and they are fun to watch.

When a beetle **larva** hatches from its egg, it does not look at all like a beetle. It is just a tiny, wiggly **grub** with six very small legs, and no sign of wings or wing cases. It eats and grows bigger, and then turns into a **pupa**.

Inside the pupa, the larva turns into a beetle. When the change is complete, the beetle comes out.

Ladybug life

1. As they grow bigger, beetle larvae shed their skins several times.

▶ Beetles lift up their wing cases and unfold a pair of thin, see-through wings to fly away from danger.

Like other insects, beetles have six legs. What makes them different is that they keep their wings folded up under a pair of hard wing cases when they are not flying around. A few beetles have no wings and cannot fly at all. These usually have long legs and can run fast to escape danger.

2. Inside a beetle pupa, the insect's body changes. Its wings and **antennae** start to grow.

3. When the beetle comes out of its pupa, it is a fully formed adult insect. This beetle is a ladybug.

Finding Beetles

Beetles live almost everywhere, except in the ocean. You will be able to find beetles in your backyard, in cities and in the countryside. Beetles live in ponds and in trees. Some are pests that live on potatoes and other crops. On a sunny day, you can find beetles eating **pollen** in flowers.

Ladybugs eat **aphids** that live on vegetables and other plants. Big, black ground beetles run along paths looking for food. If you turn over logs or rocks, you will see beetles scurrying away to hide from the light. Water beetles may lurk in ditches.

Watery whirligigs

Look for whirligigs in ponds. These small beetles swim around on the water's surface. They look silvery when they dive underwater. This is because whirligigs carry an air bubble on their bodies so they can breathe.

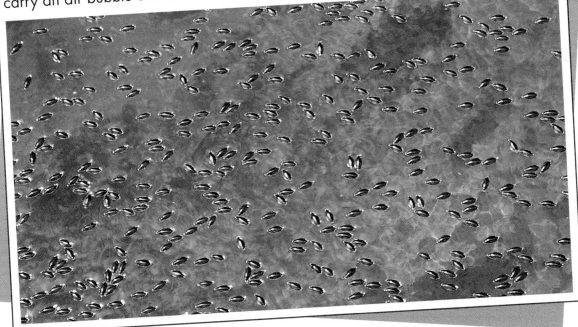

The evening is a good time to look for beetles. If it is a really warm evening, some beetles may be flying around. Many of them are attracted to light. They will collect on screen doors along with moths and other insects.

▶ The Colorado potato beetle loves to eat potatoes.

Beetle Collecting

There are several ways to catch beetles. First, you will need some containers with lids. Make small holes in the lids to let in air. You will also need some labels, a pencil, and a small, soft paintbrush.

Beetles on plants are the easiest to catch. Put a sprig of the plant they are on into a jar. Then use the paintbrush to push the beetles gently into the jar.

Remember to stick a label on each jar. Write down when and where you caught your beetle. Record details of the beetles you find in a notebook.

Beetle trap

You can make a pitfall trap to catch beetles that live on the ground. Dig a hole in the ground, and place an empty yogurt container or jelly jar in it. Add a few leaves or some soil. Beetles will fall into the trap and will be unable to climb out. Check the pot regularly, and release any insects you are not keeping as minipets.

Water beetles can be caught with a small net. Put them into a jar with plenty of water plants and some water.

It is dangerous to play near water, so make sure you go with an adult if you want to collect water beetles.

▲ When you disturb a click beetle, it will fall to the ground to escape. If it lands on its back, it will flip itself into the air with a "click" sound.

Identifying Beetles

Some beetles are very common. Others are not, so identifying them can be difficult. A book on the insects of your area will be useful, and you will soon begin to recognize different kinds.

These are some of the most common beetle families in North America. You may find many of them near where you live.

Ground beetles are black beetles that live on the ground and run fast. Some of them cannot fly.

Leaf beetles are brightly colored. Many live on trees and are hard to catch, because they just drop down if disturbed.

Weevils are often pests. They are not popular with gardeners. Weevils eat crops and stored peas and beans.

Thousands of beetles

This is a hairy bear beetle. There are so many kinds of beetles that they haven't all been counted. Some have not even been discovered yet. But there are at least 300,000 different kinds!

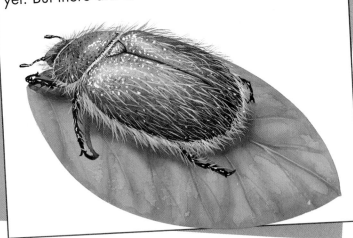

▶ Ladybugs can have lots of spots, like this seven-spotted ladybug, or none at all.

Ladybugs are well-known little beetles. They are often red, yellow, or orange with black or white spots.

Rove beetles have thin bodies and small wing cases. They feed on dead animals, **fungi**, and dead plants. Larger ones will bite.

Largest and smallest

The smallest beetles are only about the size of a pinhead. But the largest beetle is 6 inches (15 cm) long. It is the Goliath beetle (below) from central Africa.

Beetle Homes

You will need to make separate homes for each kind of beetle you collect. You can use large plastic tubs or aquariums. Try to make their homes similar to the places where you found them.

Beetles that live on the ground or under rocks need a container with soil in the bottom. Plant some small tufts of grass. Add stones and pieces of bark for hiding places.

grass

stones

soil

Ladybugs need a daily supply of fresh plants with aphids on them. Beetles that feed on pollen will need plenty of fresh flowers.

You can make an aquarium for water beetles in a glass or plastic tank. Weigh some water plants down with small rocks, and put them in. Make a raft for your water beetles by floating a piece of wood in the water.

Remember some water beetles are hunters, so you will need to add small worms or other tiny creatures as well.

Dung dwellings
Some beetles make their homes in very smelly places! There is nothing some dung beetles like better than to crawl around in cow dung.

◀ When the spotted water beetle dives underwater, it stores air in the hair under its wing cases.

Caring for Beetles

If their new homes are right for them, your beetles will be very happy. But some will be easier to look after than others. Watch your new pets carefully to see if they settle down. If they spend all their time crawling around the lid trying to get out, you will know that something is not quite right.

Always make sure your beetles have water to drink. The lid of a small jar is a good container. Try giving your beetles plain water and water with a little sugar or honey stirred in, and see which they prefer.

Beetles that come out during the day like warm sunshine. However, if you leave their container in bright sunlight, it will get far too hot inside, and the beetles will die. If you keep your beetles outside, put them somewhere sheltered from rain.

Some beetles feast on pollen or **nectar**, but their larvae need quite a different diet. Unless you know which kinds of nectar-eating beetles you have, you will not know what the female needs to lay her eggs on. It is probably best to let these beetles fly away when you have watched them for a while.

A golden wonder

An Arizona gold beetle looks like a miniature turtle. The female protects her eggs with her golden shell. The larvae protect themselves by carrying an "umbrella" around them, made of their own droppings!

Feeding Beetles

It is not always easy to find the right food for every kind of beetle. Some beetles do not eat at all. They do all their feeding when they are grubs. But most beetles eat something, even if it is only nectar from flowers.

If you are not sure what your beetle eats, put small amounts of different foods in its home. Then the beetle can decide. Good things to try are slices of apple or cucumber. For meat-eating beetles, a tiny bit of cat or dog food may work.

Some beetles are quite fierce hunters. They will need other live bugs to catch and eat. If you want to keep these beetles, you will have to go hunting for their food.

Use the pitfall trap that you made to catch your beetles. You can use the tiny **invertebrates** you catch as food for your hungry beetle.

▼ This weevil eats the wood of pine and spruce trees.

Wood-eaters

Wood-boring beetles have larvae that spend their time eating wood. As they chew, they leave a tunnel behind them. The wood is not very nutritious. It may take 3 years or longer before the larvae have grown enough to turn into adult beetles.

Protecting Themselves

A beetle's tough suit of armor protects it from many enemies. But even big, well-protected beetles are still eaten by owls and bats.

Some beetles have extra ways to make sure they do not end up as a snack. Ground beetles and darkling beetles have bad smells to put off enemies. Blister beetles release oily blood when they are attacked. This causes painful blisters if it gets onto the skin of people, birds, or other animals.

Ladybugs taste awful, and their bright colors warn birds not to peck them up.

▶ Some harmless beetles just pretend to be creatures that can bite or sting. This beetle looks just like a wasp.

Beetle bombers

Bombardier beetles really use chemical warfare! When attacked, they shoot boiling hot liquids and gases from their **abdomen** into the enemy's face.

Water beetles use their sharp jaws to give enemies a nip. Diving beetles are some of the fiercest meat-eating beetles. Both the adults and larvae eat tadpoles and even small fish!

▼ Tiger beetles escape from danger either by running or flying away very fast.

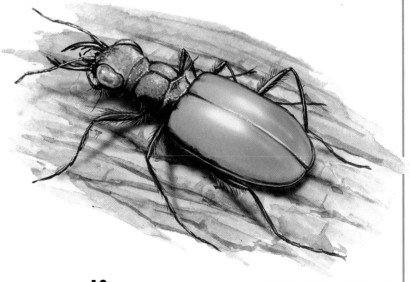

Multiplying Beetles

Beetles have to pair up in order to multiply. They find their mates by sight, sound, or smell. Quite often, beetles meet at their feeding places.

▲ Ladybugs lay their eggs in clusters near aphid-infested leaves.

You may find a beetle laying eggs when you are out beetle-hunting. Carefully pick the plant with eggs on it, and put the stem in a jar of water.

Check every day to see if the eggs have hatched. The hatched larvae will not look at all like the parent beetles.

Put the tiny larvae on some fresh leaves of the same plant in a container with airholes. You could take notes on their development until they finally **pupate** and emerge as adult beetles.

Food for the family

Burying beetles like the sexton beetle dig the soil beneath a small, dead animal away until it sinks into the ground. Then they lay their eggs next to the dead body, so that the larvae can feed on it.

Hot and Cold

When winter comes, beetles grow scarce. Some wiggle under logs and rocks. Others go down into the ground where frosts cannot reach them. They stay there until the cold weather passes. But many kinds die, leaving their larvae to spend the winter in logs or in other sheltered places.

Ladybugs often **hibernate** in the dead, hollow stems of plants. Ask an adult to slit the stems open carefully so you can have a look. You may find many in a cluster. They do not move or eat until the warm weather comes.

▼ Thirteen-spotted ladybugs gather together in large numbers to hibernate.

If you uncover hibernating beetles, make sure you put them somewhere free of frost after you have counted them and taken notes.

Beetles also live in some of the world's hottest, driest deserts. They hide in the sand by day, and emerge to feed only at night. Desert beetles often have very long legs. These keep the insect's body off the hot sand, and allow it to run very fast. Desert beetles get most of their water from dew in the early mornings.

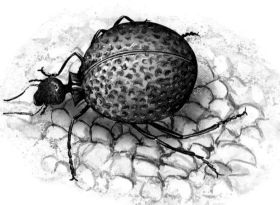

▲ Desert blister beetles live in the southwestern United States.

Wearing white

A desert darkling beetle from Namibia in Southern Africa is very unusual because it has pure white wing cases. These help it keep cool by reflecting the sun's heat.

Keeping a Record

Keeping a scrapbook will give you an interesting record of beetle behavior. You can also keep a record of beetles you see in the wild, but do not collect. Draw a picture of them, and find out what they are.

You could record when each species appears. Some come out in the spring. But others, such as chafers and stag beetles, only emerge in the summer.

BEETLES

Found: Under a stone
Date: August 28
I kept this beetle in a jar to draw it. It was a quarter of an inch (6 mm) long.

This is a photo of a beetle we found in the forest.

The shiny red parts of this ladybug are its wing cases.

You can paste pictures from magazines into your scrapbook. Many **tropical** beetles, in particular, are large and colorful.

You could join a wildlife club, or start a beetle club with some of your friends. You can find out more about beetles from the library or at a natural history museum.

Giant jaws

There's no mistaking a stag beetle. It has enormous jaws, especially the male. They use their jaws for wrestling with other males. They cannot pinch very hard with them. However, the smaller jaws of the female stag beetle can give quite a nip.

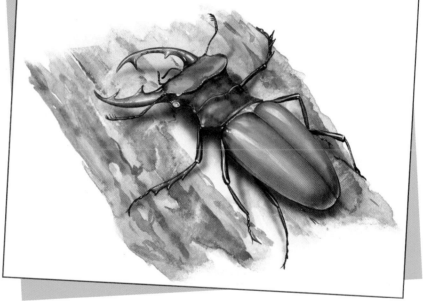

When you get to know beetles a little better, you may decide to specialize in one group of these fascinating insects. For instance, you could study water beetles or beetles that live in the trees near your home. You could even study beetle pests. You will soon become a beetle expert!

Letting Them Go

Some adult beetles only live for a few days or weeks. After they have laid their eggs, their job is done, and they die. But others live for years, so you could have your pets for a long time.

When you have finished watching your pets, it is best to let them go. Check in your notebook to see where you found them, and take them back to the same place. If they are **nocturnal** beetles, release them in the evening. If they are beetles that fly in the day, let them go on a warm morning. Be sure to leave beetle eggs or larvae where there will be enough to eat.

▶ This violet ground beetle can live for a year or longer as an adult.

Wherever you go, you are almost sure to find new beetles. Some of these live in homes you could not easily make yourself, such as in streams, deep in wet moss, or inside a large toadstool.

Always take a hand lens with you to watch these tiny beetles as they scurry all around.

Light at night

Fireflies are beetles that use their own flashing lights to find each other. Each kind has its own code of flashes. They only come out at night, so their signals show clearly like flashlights in the dark.

Beetle Facts

The golden beetle is a rare beetle from Costa Rica. It is quite large, and its wing cases are a bright, shiny, gold color.

▼ Golden beetle

The violin beetle is flat with side flaps around its body. These flaps make it appear as though it is shaped like a violin. It lives in Indonesia.

Dung beetles called scarabs were sacred to the ancient Egyptians. The scarabs symbolized their sun god, Ra. They even made some scarabs into jewelry.

The male giraffe-necked weevil from Madagascar is one of the oddest-looking insects. It has an elongated "neck" and head with eyes, mouth, and antennae right at the tip!

The male Hercules beetle (or rhinoceros beetle) has enormous "horns" on its head and **thorax**, up to 3 inches (8 cm) long. Hercules beetles use their horns to wrestle with rival males.

There are many kinds of longhorn beetles. Some tropical species are large, with very long antennae. Longhorn larvae feed on wood. Before laying her eggs on a tree trunk, the female makes sure it is large enough to provide food for her larvae.

◀ Horse-bean longhorn beetle

Further Reading

Crewe, Sabrina. *The Ladybug* (Life Cycles series). Raintree Steck-Vaughn, 1997.

Fisher, Enid. *Beetles*. Gareth Stevens, 1996.

Murray, Peter. *Beetles*. Child's World, 1993.

Parker, Steve. *Beastly Bugs*. Raintree Steck-Vaughn, 1994.

Zeifert, Harriet. *Bugs, Beetles, and Butterflies*. Viking, 1998.